EX
LIBRIS

Top 10 Worst

Vicious Villains

you wouldn't want to know!

Sandy Creek
NEW YORK

An Imprint of Sterling Publishing
387 Park Avenue South
New York, NY 10016

Series creator: David Salariya
Author: Jim Pipe
Editor: Jamie Pitman
Illustrations: David Antram

ISBN 978-1-4351-5043-0 (HB)

Manufactured in Heshan, Guangdong Province, China
Lot #:
2 4 6 8 10 9 7 5 3 1
06/13

Top 10 Worst™

Vicious Villains

you wouldn't want to know!

Created & designed by
David Salariya

Illustrated by
David Antram

Written by
Jim Pipe

Sandy Creek
NEW YORK

Contents

What is a villain?

A villain is someone who carries out wicked acts or crimes. The word "villain" probably makes you think of the bad guys in movies and books, but throughout history there have been plenty of real-life people willing to rob and murder. Often violent thugs—both men and women—they have been given all sorts of different names:

Gunslinger

Highwayman

Bandit

Gangster

Outlaw

Bushranger

I'm the most vicious varmint in these here parts! So stick 'em up!

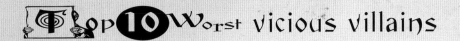

Who becomes a villain?

Villains carry out foul deeds for all sorts of different reasons. Most highwaymen, gangsters, bandits, and outlaws robbed just to get rich. The Thuggees of India killed their victims to honor the goddess Kali, while the not-so-noble Borgias wanted to bump off their political rivals. Though Sawney Bean murdered lonely travelers to feed his family, Countess Elizabeth Báthory killed just for fun!

Common gossip would spread the word of heroes and villains, as their lives made for exciting stories.

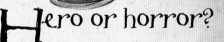
Robin Hood

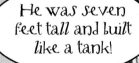
He was seven feet tall and built like a tank!

Hero or horror?

The word "outlaw" conjures up images of daring heroes such as Robin Hood, who in legend stole money from the rich to give to the poor. But in medieval versions of the story, he is a common murderer! When Guy Fawkes tried to blow up the English parliament buildings in 1605, he was called Robin Hood as an insult.

Made-up villains

Some famous fictional villains have been based on real-life criminals. Professor James Moriarty, detective Sherlock Holmes' archenemy, was based on a real London gang leader called Adam Worth, nicknamed the "Napoleon of Crime." During the 1870s, he organized a string of major robberies, but British detectives were never able to pin anything on him.

Just a good story?

It can be hard to tell fact from fiction when it comes to villains. In reality, bandits and outlaws were usually vicious criminals. Over the years, storytellers and songwriters made up stories, and each time they were told, the tales got more fantastic. That said, it's no wonder that so many stories have been written about villains. They certainly lived colorful, action-packed lives: chasing, fighting, hiding, and escaping from the law.

So why was he called Little John?

Gossip!

Chitchat!

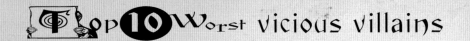

Where do villains lurk?

Crime knows no frontiers. Where there are people to be robbed and possessions to be taken, there are villains lurking in the shadows!

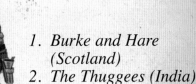

10

8

6

1. Burke and Hare (Scotland)
2. The Thuggees (India)
3. The Borgias (Italy)
4. The Blood Countess (Hungary)
5. Sawney Bean (Scotland)
6. Jesse James (USA)
7. Ned Kelly (Australia)
8. Billy the Kid (USA)
9. Dick Turpin (England)
10. Al Capone (USA)

Villains often do nasty things to other people, so why are they so fascinating? Perhaps it's the dangerous adventures they have, which inspire us to make up our own stories. Or maybe we just wonder what it would be like to meet them face-to-face?

Cyber~villains

These days, villains don't have to meet their victims to hurt them. Criminal gangs try to rob their victims using the Internet or even mobile phones, so it's important to be careful when using these devices.

4

3

2

7

This book tells the stories of ten of the world's most vicious villains. But there have been thousands of others, in every country in the world. Maybe a famous historical rogue once lived near you!

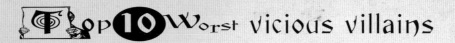

No 10

Al Capone

Nicknamed "Scarface" after getting slashed during a fight, Al Capone was the most feared gangster in America during the 1920s and 1930s. His gang, the "Capones," made their money from smuggling alcohol, which was illegal during the Prohibition years. They often battled other mobs in Chicago. Capone ordered the murder of many rivals and even killed some of them with his own hands.

Vital Statistics

Name: Alphonse "Al" Gabriel Capone

Alias: "Scarface"

Lived: 1899 to 1947

Crimes: Murder, smuggling, tax evasion

Victims: Dozens of rival gangsters

You wouldn't want to know this:

One of the Capones' victims took three hours to die. When asked who shot him, he replied, "Nobody," despite having 14 bullet wounds!

When Capone found out members of his own gang were out to get him, he bashed them with a baseball bat, then had them shot.

Are you looking at me, wise guy?

Be prepared!
Always expect the very worst

St. Valentine's Day massacre

In 1929, Capone hoped to ambush a rival gangster, Bugs Moran. On February 14, St. Valentine's Day, five members of Moran's North Side gang and two other men turned up at a garage expecting to buy illegal drink. Dressed as police officers, Capone's mobsters lined them up against the wall—and gunned them down in a hail of bullets.

In the slammer

In 1929, FBI agent Eliot Ness began to investigate Capone. Two years later, Capone was finally sentenced to 11 years in prison—for not paying his taxes!

Nicknames

Guess how these gangsters got their nicknames: Jimmy the Gent, Terry "Machine Gun" Druggan, Vincent "Mad Dog" Coll, and Donald Angelini, "The Wizard of Odds." Tough guy "Lucky" Luciano got his nickname after getting his throat cut, being left for dead in a ditch, and somehow surviving!

Capone spent much of his time behind bars in the notorious Alcatraz prison in San Francisco Bay.

> Making a swim for it?

Secret weapons

POSSE BENT ON LYNCHING
SEARCHES WOODS FOR PREY

Chicago Defender

There's a popular myth that gangsters carried their machine guns in violin cases. It's probably untrue, but they did hide them: Capone kept a shotgun in a golf bag, while other mobsters hid them under folded newspapers.

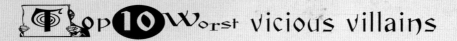

No 9

Dick Turpin

If you believe the legends, "Dauntless" Dick Turpin was a handsome hero. Riding his noble steed Black Bess, he dashed along highways, robbing the rich and winning the hearts of ladies. The real Richard Turpin was a regular thief who tortured his female victims until they handed over their money and jewelry.

Contrary to legend, Dick Turpin's famous ride, from London to York in less than 24 hours, was actually made by 17th-century highwayman John "Swift Nick" Nevison.

Vital statistics

Name: Richard Turpin
Alias: "Gentleman Highwayman"
Lived: c.1705 to 1739
Crimes: Highway robbery, burglary, stealing horses and sheep
Victims: He tortured many.

You wouldn't want to know this:

When a wealthy widow refused to tell Turpin where her money was hidden, he hoisted her over an open fire until she gave up her treasure.

Catch me if you can!

Gallop!

Be prepared!
Always expect the very worst

Stand and deliver!

The sheep stealer

Young Turpin started out stealing sheep and cattle to sell in his butcher's shop. After he was found out, he fled into the countryside where he formed the Essex Gang. The gang attacked farmhouses and robbed the inhabitants. Later, Turpin began working with "Captain" Tom King, a famous highwayman. From a hidden cave in Epping Forest, they robbed passersby.

A graceful exit

One night, lawmen tracked Turpin and King to a London pub. In the fight, Turpin accidentally shot his partner! Turpin headed north to York, where he was eventually arrested for stealing horses. Only on his way to the gallows did Turpin act like a hero, bowing to the crowds and chatting to his executioner.

The wicked lady

Highwaymen were mounted robbers who held up stagecoaches. Some did have a romantic streak: Frenchman Claude Duval danced with a lady during a holdup near London in 1668. Lady Catherine Ferrers, known as the "Wicked Lady," robbed coaches just for fun. After many daring holdups, she was finally shot by one of her victims in 1660.

Click!

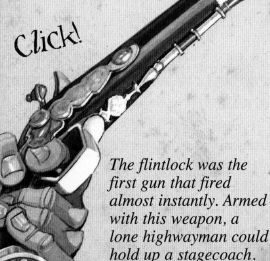

The flintlock was the first gun that fired almost instantly. Armed with this weapon, a lone highwayman could hold up a stagecoach.

Your money or your life!

13

No 8

Billy the Kid

Henry McCarty, or "Billy the Kid," was a brutal Wild West outlaw who killed several men while still a teenager. Soon he was one of the most wanted men in the West. After his capture at Stinking Springs in 1880, he told a reporter: "People thought me bad before, but if I ever get free, I'll let them know what bad means." He became a legend after his captor, Sheriff Pat Garrett, wrote a best-selling book about him.

Vital Statistics

Name: Henry McCarty
Alias: William Bonney or "Billy the Kid"
Lived: 1859 to 1881
Crimes: Cattle rustling, murder, gambling
Victims: Murdered 4–9 people

You wouldn't want to know this:

While escaping from prison, Billy grabbed a shotgun, then lay in wait for his captors. When deputy Robert Ollinger came running past, Billy shouted, "Hello, Bob!" Then he blasted him with the shotgun. Billy then rode out of town, reportedly singing.

Come on, I'll take you all on!

Be prepared!
Always expect the very worst

Dead or alive

In the wide open spaces of the Wild West, it wasn't always easy to capture villains. So criminals were made into "outlaws." This meant anyone could bring them in: "Dead or Alive." Most were robbers or murderers. Some, such as Butch Cassidy, were turned into heroes in books and films.

WANTED
DEAD OR ALIVE
$1,000

Woah!

Bang!

In cold blood

It's said that Billy carried out his first murder at just 12, stabbing a man in a saloon fight. Later, when his ranch boss was killed in a gang feud, Billy set out on a bloody trail of murder and cattle rustling.

Eventually Billy was hunted down by Sheriff Pat Garrett to a house in New Mexico. Garrett ambushed Billy and shot him dead. Billy was just 21.

Son of a gun!

Many Wild West outlaws had nicknames, like "Big Nose" George Parrot or Thomas "Black Jack" Ketchum, while Harvey Logan was called "Kid Curry." Gangs had names as well. Billy the Kid was one of the Regulators. Butch Cassidy and the Sundance Kid (real names Robert Leroy Parker and Harry Longbaugh) were members of the Wild Bunch.

It was a race to draw our guns – and I got there first!

I can sniff danger a mile off!

15

No 9

Ned Kelly

Ned Kelly is Australia's most famous bandit. Although he was a bank robber who shot several policemen, some say he was only defending himself. The Kelly gang famously built suits of bulletproof armor. When the police first saw it, one of them cried out, "Look out, boys, it's the bunyip," referring to a mythical lake monster. But Kelly's armor did not save him from the hangman. His last words were: "Such is life!"

Vital Statistics

Name: Edward Kelly
Alias: "Ned"
Lived: 1855 to 1880
Crimes: Cattle rustling, murder, robbery
Victims: He shot three dead.

You wouldn't want to know this:

The Kelly gang often took hostages who were only set free if their demands were met. In the final shoot-out, several hostages were shot, and three died, including 13-year-old Jack Jones. But on another occasion, the outlaws entertained their prisoners with a display of horse riding and tricks.

Give it your best shot. I'm bulletproof!

Be prepared!
Always expect the very worst

Bushrangers

Australia's most feared bandits were the bushrangers. Most were convicts or outlaws who had escaped into the bush, Australia's wilderness. They robbed farmers and travelers with the cry "Bail up!" This meant "halt," as cows were held still by putting bails (frames) around their neck.

Robin Hoods?

Nineteenth century songs called ballads made the bushrangers into brave heroes. Ned Kelly and Frederick Ward, alias "Captain Thunderbolt," were seen as Robin Hoods, robbing from the rich to help the poor. Captain Thunderbolt, famous for his fast horse, preferred to escape from trouble rather than get into a shoot-out.

Zoom!

Bail up!

On the run

As a young man, Ned Kelly often got into trouble with the police. Accused of wounding a police officer, Ned, his brother, and two friends fled into the bush. When the police tracked him down, Ned shot three of them dead. His gang were now outlaws. He led them in two bank raids, sharing the money with his family and neighbors.

When the police finally caught up with the Kelly gang on June 28, 1880, they fired 15,000 bullets into the inn where the gang were hiding. The bullets bounced off Kelly's armor until he was shot in the legs. He was arrested and hanged for murder soon afterward.

Sorry, it's for the mammy!

17

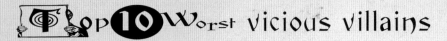

No 6

Jesse James

One of the most notorious outlaws of the Wild West was Jesse James. In 1867, he robbed his first bank, and six years later his gang held up their first train. He once held up two stagecoaches in one day. Many poor farmers hated the banks and railroads he stole from, so Jesse James became a legend. But was he really such a hero?

Vital Statistics

Name: Jesse Woodson James
Alias: "Dingus"
Lived: 1847 to 1882
Crimes: Horse stealing, train and bank robbery, murder
Victims: 14 dead

You wouldn't want to know this:

A five-year-old girl was once trampled to death while Jesse James was robbing a ticket booth at the Missouri State Fair.

Tickets, please!

Be prepared!
Always expect the very worst

Blown sky-high!

Train robbers often picked a quiet spot where the train slowed down. Riding up on horses, one of them jumped onto the moving train, then unhitched the railcars with the loot in them. Once, the Wild Bunch used too much dynamite to crack the safe. They blew up the whole car, sending $30,000 in cash into the air!

Room for two

Jesse James first became famous in 1869 after he robbed a bank in Gallatin, Missouri, and killed the cashier. Now outlaws, Jesse and his brother Frank made a daring escape by riding off on the same horse.

A bungled job

During a raid on Northfield, Minnesota, in 1876, the cashiers refused to hand over the money. Outside, five of the James gang were shot in a gun battle with the locals. But James soon formed a new gang. In 1881, he robbed four more trains.

Soon Jesse's new gang fell out and the only people he trusted were two brothers, Charley and Robert Ford. Bad move. Bob shot Jesse in the head while he was hanging a picture, then claimed the reward!

Sorry, Jesse.

Click!

No 5

Sawney Bean

Sawney Bean was a Scottish bandit said to live with his large family in a cave by the sea. For 25 years, their supplies came from robbing passing travelers at night—and their food came from eating them! The Beans were sneaky. They never attacked more than two travelers at a time, then they mobbed their victims so there was no escape.

Vital Statistics

Name: Alexander "Sawney" Bean
Alias: "The Cannibal Bandit"
Lived: 16th century
Crimes: Robbery, murder
Victims: Many

You wouldn't want to know this:

Legend says that Sawney Bean was the head of a cursed tribe of killers, including his wife, eight sons, six daughters, 18 grandsons and 14 granddaughters!

Something I ate disagreed with me!

Yes, your last victim!

Be prepared!
Always expect the very worst

The Donner Party

There have been several cases of people eating each other when supplies ran low. In the winter of 1846–1847, a group of American pioneers known as the Donner (not dinner!) Party resorted to eating each other after getting caught in the snow in the Sierra Nevada mountains of California.

Gosh! Something's afoot!

After murdering their victims, the Beans brought the bodies back to the cave and cut them up. Leftover parts were sometimes thrown into the sea. When the tide washed up arms and legs, people wondered who had carried out this terrible crime.

I hope you smell 'em before I do!

Sniff

When the tide was in, the water flowed deep into the Beans' cave, so no one knew anyone lived there.

Napkin, anyone?

Caught red-handed!

One night, a group of fairgoers caught the Beans in the middle of an ambush. King James VI of Scotland is said to have sent out 400 men and several bloodhounds, who found the Beans' cave littered with human remains. The whole family was taken away and executed!

No 4

The Blood Countess

One of the cruelest women who ever lived, the Hungarian countess Elizabeth Báthory is said to have killed dozens if not hundreds of young women. Rumors spread that Báthory was a vampire who drank her victims' blood as well as bathing in it. Both stories are probably untrue. She was just a vicious villain who was rich and powerful enough to get away with murder.

Vital statistics

Name: Countess Elizabeth Báthory de Ecsed
Alias: The "Blood Countess"
Lived: 1560 to 1614
Crimes: Murder, torture
Victims: Between 80 and 650, no one knows for sure!

You wouldn't want to know this:

In one version of the story, Báthory's husband, who was away at war, sent tips on how to kill her victims. One charming idea was to cover them in honey so they would be bitten to death by hungry insects.

There's nothing like a good soak!

That's so sweet of him

Be prepared!
Always expect the very worst

Kidnapped!

Báthory's victims were often teenage girls from poor families. They were lured to her castles at Csejte and Sárvár by offers of well-paid work as maids. She was helped by four servants, who also kidnapped girls from the surrounding countryside.

Now this *is* what I call "blood money."

Vlad the Impaler

Chomp!

A hundred years earlier, Vlad III, Prince of Wallachia (1431–1476), got the nickname "Impaler" after forcing a sharp stake into the bodies of 30,000 captured enemies. He was also known as Dracula, meaning the "Son of the Dragon." The name was later used by writer Bram Stoker for his famous vampire Dracula.

Let off the hook

So many girls disappeared near Báthory's castle that the local governor is said to have led a raid on the castle and arrested everyone inside. One girl was found in the hall, dead and drained of blood. Many others were found locked up in the dungeons. Báthory was a rich countess, so no one dared to execute her. She was walled up in a room in her castle, and died there four years later.

I never touched her—honest!

№3

The Borgias

The Borgias were a power-mad Spanish family famous for committing murder and mayhem after moving to Rome in the mid-1400s. Their favorite trick was to invite wealthy rivals to dinner, poison them, and rob them of their property. They weren't the only vicious rulers, though. In England, King Henry VIII beheaded two of his wives, while French King Louis XI wove so many plots he was known as the "Spider King."

Vital Statistics

Name: Borgias (Italy) or de Borjas (Spain)

Alias: Cesare was known as "Valentino" and Rodrigo as the "petticoat cardinal"

In power: 1492 to 1507

Crimes: Murder, bribery, robbery

Victims: At least a dozen

You wouldn't want to know this:

The Borgias were said to have concocted a special recipe for poisoning their rivals, a deadly blend of arsenic and phosphorus known as *cantarella*.

Cesare

Lucrezia

Chuckle

Guffaw

Rodrigo

> I think the wine is off, darling!

24

Be prepared!
Always expect the very worst

Toxic times

Poisoning was all the rage in Renaissance times. There were many textbooks written describing how to create the perfect poison, and the streets of Paris were filled with professional poisoners. Toffana, a woman from Naples in Italy, even created a special poison for wives who wanted to bump off their husbands.

Ruthless rulers

Rodrigo Borgia was elected Pope Alexander VI in 1492—after buying most of the votes. To make themselves more powerful, Rodrigo and his children accused rich nobles and church leaders of crimes, then flung them in jail or killed them. The Duke of Gandia's body was found floating in the Tiber River in Rome, probably murdered by Cesare Borgia.

Drip!

Why? Because I'm the Pope... and I say so!

Brotherly love

Glimmer

Most ruthless of the Borgias was Cesare, who killed anyone who got in his way, possibly even his elder brother, Giovanni. This killer streak was admired by the famous writer and philosopher Niccolò Macchiavelli.

The poison beauty

Rodrigo's daughter Lucrezia had a ring that was hollowed out in the middle and contained a dose of poison. Her first husband fled after her father ordered his murder, while her second was strangled by her brother Cesare's men.

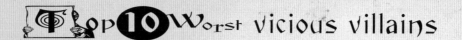

No 2

The Thuggees

Throughout history, bands of vicious bandits have lain in wait to ambush travelers, such as the brigands that plagued Europe in medieval times. During the 1800s, Indian bandits known as *thuggees* killed countless travelers as a sacrifice to Kali, a Hindu goddess. They were so fearsome they gave the world a new word: "thug."

Vital Statistics

Name:
Alias: Thuggees "Stranglers" or "Noose operators"
Active: 16th to 19th centuries
Crimes: Murder, robbery
Victims: 50,000 to 2 million

You wouldn't want to know this:

The Thuggees believed they had to kill their victims without spilling any blood, so they strangled them. This was quick and quiet and didn't alert other travelers sleeping nearby. The bodies were then buried or thrown into a nearby well.

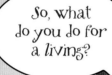

So, what do you do for a living?

Oh, you'll see...

Whistle!

Be prepared!
Always expect the very worst

A world of bandits

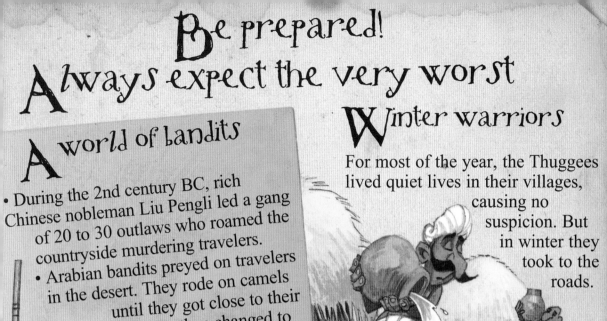

• During the 2nd century BC, rich Chinese nobleman Liu Pengli led a gang of 20 to 30 outlaws who roamed the countryside murdering travelers.

• Arabian bandits preyed on travelers in the desert. They rode on camels until they got close to their victims, then changed to ponies for a burst of speed.

• During the 1250s, a group of robber barons in Germany attacked boats sailing up the Rhine river, grabbing whole ships and kidnapping those on board. They were known as the *Raubritter,* or "thieving knights."

Winter warriors

For most of the year, the Thuggees lived quiet lives in their villages, causing no suspicion. But in winter they took to the roads.

The Thuggees' usual tactic was to join a group of traveling merchants. After winning the trust of the other merchants, they robbed and killed them in a surprise night attack, choosing a place such as a riverbank where it was hard for their victims to escape.

Mass murder

When the time was right, a secret signal was given, and the thuggees sprang into action. Each member of the gang had a job. Some distracted the victims or did the strangling. Others acted as lookouts or guarded the campsite so no one escaped. The Thuggee code said the bandits couldn't kill women, blind people, or carpenters, but they still murdered thousands of travelers each year.

Glark!

Stop! I'm a whiz with a saw and hammer—and I'm blind!

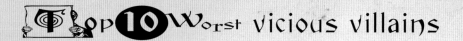

No 1

Burke and Hare

In the early 19th century, two Irish laborers, Burke and Hare, came to Edinburgh, Scotland, looking for work. They discovered they could make money by selling corpses to Dr. Robert Knox, a surgeon who wanted to show his students the marvels of the human body. People were outraged when they heard that body snatchers were digging up fresh graves. Burke and Hare went one step further, murdering their victims to order.

It seems very fresh!

Vital Statistics

Name: William Burke (1792–1829) and William Hare (dates unknown)

Active: November 1827 to October 1828

Crimes: Murder, theft

Victims: Between 17 and 30 killed

You wouldn't want to know this:

Burke and Hare killed many of their victims by getting them drunk, then smothering them—a murder method forever after known as "burking." This left no mark on the victims. Hare finished off one small boy by putting him over his knee and breaking his back.

Be prepared!
Always expect the very worst

Bodysnatchers

In the 1820s, Edinburgh was *the* place to study medicine. Doctors could cut up the corpses of criminals to show their students how a body works. But there were never enough bodies to go around. So criminals dug up dead bodies from graveyards, then sold them to doctors.

Gasp!

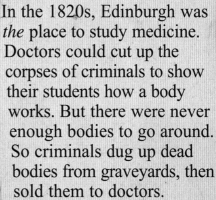

This way!

Unlike other body snatchers, Burke and Hare were murderers, picking on easy targets without family or friends. Their victims included elderly pensioners, the poor and homeless, and a young boy. Hare's wife, Margaret, and Burke's girlfriend, Helen, lured victims off the street to Margaret's lodging house.

Bump in the night!

Burke and Hare were found out when two lodgers, James and Ann Gray, heard strange noises in the night and told the police. The next day, the Grays found a victim's body under a bed. The deadly duo were arrested. Burke was tried and hanged while Hare was released for giving evidence agaist Burke. After his death, Burke's body was cut open in public, just like his victims. His skeleton and skin are still on display in Edinburgh.

Another day at the office, eh?

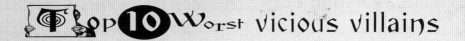

Glossary

Bandit An armed thief who robs others, often in the countryside.

Body snatcher Someone who steals dead bodies from their graves, also called a grave robber.

Bushranger A bandit living in the wilderness of the Australian bush.

Cannibal Someone who eats human flesh.

Captor A person who captures someone else.

Cattle rustling Stealing cattle.

Convict Someone serving a prison sentence. In the 18th and 19th centuries, many British convicts were shipped to Australia.

Corpse The dead body of a human or animal.

Criminal Someone guilty of carrying out a serious crime.

Dynamite A type of explosive.

Executioner Someone who carries out a death sentence.

FBI The United States' Federal Bureau of Investigation, an agency that combats organized crime.

Flintlock A type of early gun. A flint in the gun's hammer made a spark that set off the gunpowder.

Gallows The nickname for the wooden frame used to hang criminals in past times.

Gangster A criminal who belongs to a gang.

Gunslinger A hired killer who uses a gun.

Highwayman A robber on horseback from the 17th and 18th centuries who preyed on travelers, especially those in stagecoaches.

Hostage Someone held against their will.

Illegal Against the law.

Kali The Hindu goddess of time, energy, and destruction.

Legend A traditional tale that contains bits of history but may not be completely true.

Lodger Someone who occupies a room in a house, usually for a fee.

Massacre A terrible slaughter of human beings, using weapons.

Medieval Belonging to the Middle Ages, the period from AD 400 to AD 1500.

Mobster A gangster.

Murder To kill someone on purpose.

Outlaw Someone who lives outside the law, such as a bandit or highwayman.

Parliament The government of a country or the buildings it meets in.

Pioneers The first settlers in a new land.

Pope The head of the Roman Catholic church.

Prohibition A period in United States history when it was illegal to produce or sell alcohol (from 1920 to 1933).

Renaissance A period that saw a great revival of art in Europe (from the 14th to the 16th centuries).

Saloon A bar in the American Wild West that sold drinks to cowboys, trappers, and soldiers.

Smuggling Bringing illegal goods into a country, usually in secret.

Stagecoach A large coach used to carry passengers and mail on regular routes between towns.

Tax evasion Not paying your taxes on purpose.

Wild West The American West in the 19th century, usually meaning anywhere west of the Mississippi River.

Index

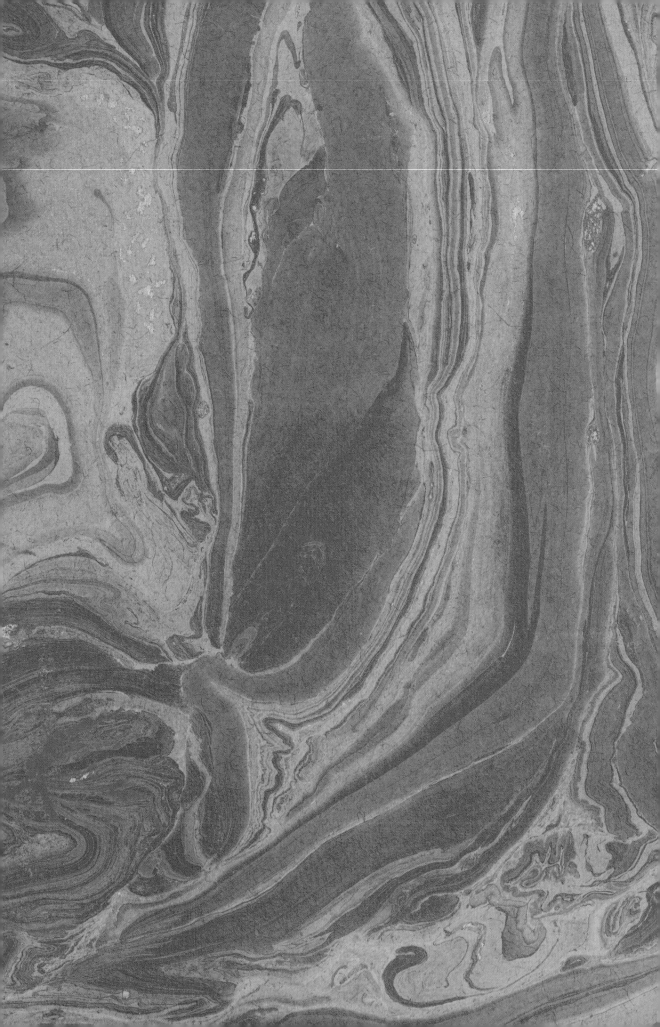